Publishing Independently

Are Typos and Getting Reviews a Big Deal?

Loran Joly

Copyright © 2023 by Loran Joly

All rights reserved.

No portion of this book may be reproduced in any form without written permission from the publisher or author, except as permitted by U.S. copyright law.

Contents

Why I Publish Books With Typos & No Reviews   IV

Dedication   VI

Publishing Woes?   1

More Difficulties in Publishing   3

About the Author   7

To contact the author....   17

Refund policy   19

Why I Publish Books With Typos & No Reviews

North Carolina

image by author

To my parents, who made this possible.

For instance, my mother, an immigrant from eastern
Poland, having come to America at the age of twelve,
after a two week long boat journey, to Ellis Island....

*My mother as a young gal in Europe, before
coming to America*

And to my father, too, a most astute Trainer in life....

Brought up in the ghettos of Philadelphia; left school at

the age of seventeen; and later acquired a GED and went

on to obtain a Ph.D. degree at a major University in Eng-
lish Literature; who thus led to my interest and pursuit
of writing at a very early age; and too, with respect to his
love of photography, both of these areas, too, rubbing off
on me: hence, "The apple doesn't fall far from the tree"?

Training!

Publishing Woes?

Some Kingpin critical reasons why a very few might want to publish **WITH NO REVIEWS** and **NO TESTIMONIALS!**

To publish truths spoken respectfully, if NOONE ELSE CAN – in a certain area - and thus IS doing.

And on many topics, not just one or two.

And brilliantly.

And with views coming from outside of normal channels.

And when the person doesn't have the time or energy or health to seek these reviews.

Or when they're committed to an ailing loved one or have children they're committed to also.

Or committed in general to caretaking an elderly parent or parents.

Or when their morals prevent them from getting money for editors because they won't do what it takes to get those monies.

More Difficulties in Publishing

Hence, some having sparse funds due to morals.
Considering, say, that Thomas Gore died supposedly poor in an oil-rich State because he wouldn't take graft.

Or when the individual can't demonstrate their product in person as per speaking.

Or too, because the person is too envied for the assets that made the person who they are – assets which you can't just get by signing up to a great college or even say, Navy SEAL training.

Or, because TOO MANY feel their OMNISCIENCE too DASHED, by the ingisht – level of VIEWS, in COMPARISON to THEIR level of Knowledge.

Or, because TOO MANY feel NO LONGER #1 as per THEMSELVES, or their GROUP to be #1.

***

Noting, that these persons CAN MUDDLE BY, for some time, PERHAPS even UNTIL their DEATHBED, WITHOUT absolutely needing the information of that "Key Insightful": PREFERING to "CUT OFF their NOSE to SPITE the Person".

Or because they're physically ill.

Or because the material is considered so controversial that many won't help the individual unless the person looks extremely viable.

Or because they have no spouse nor children to help them.

Or because they live in an area of the country where the infrastructure is very poor.

OR, because GETTING the FIRST FEW to SIGN ON to ANY "MOVEMENT" is VERY HARD:

AND LIKEWISE, for GETTING REVIEWS, and SUBSCRIBERS to their YOUTUBE Channels, say.

About the Author

The author resides in Kentucky,

The author does not have a Ph.D. or an MD degree. Nor is he a college graduate – for he does not consider his four years at West Point to be a college, and his four years at Berea College, studying solely athematics, were as a community member at the half time level, and no degree was ever thus awarded....

***

These are some of his credentials....

The author's influences include ...

Key aspects of the author's life have included...

Last day at West Point in 1983

Author, left; aunt - middle, who was key to my growing by telling me I needed to get into therapy .. she lived in Beverly Hills and was in the entertainment industry, so a year later, I did .. psychoanalysis, with a physician at a local medical school in Kentucky, and continuing on a year later in San Diego, California; and cousin, right, in California, a few years after my time in the Army in Germany

My violins: the closest one was purchased and carried on my father's back as he travelled in Germany. I started Suzuki violin lessons in North Carolina at the age of seven, and later studied at The MacPhail Center For Music in Minneapolis, Minnesota, when our family moved there in 1970 when I was ten; in eleventh grade, I played in a local college orchestra, and in my senior year, I took violin lessons at the University of Kentucky from a violin professor, and played in the Central Kentucky Youth Symphony Orchestra, practicing my violin at home, two hours a day, seven days a week. It was my hope to be

*Berea College grounds, where I was the Pon-
derer of the Math department, studying only
mathematics at the ages of forty-one through
forty-five, and tutoring for the Berea College
Mathematics Department, to pay off all my
tuition at this scholarship-only college. Here
I first learned to use a computer; and purchased my first cellphone: both at the young
age of forty-one...*

It was here that I continued my photography work, and including joining the local photo club, where I met a Mr. Warren Brunner, the town's portrait photographer, who I reconnected with in 2021 and was greatly encouraged by; he was instrumental in my future photo efforts, and a year after meeting with him frequently in 2021 and during 2022, I first started keeping a portfolio of images on Fine Art America's website; and then, started creating photo books on places in Kentucky; and then started a Shopify store in late 2022, too, to sell these.

One of many buildings at Berea College

*Photograph of my moth-
er, left, at the age of two;
my grandmother, center,
and a helper, right, 1940,
as war refugees in Poland,
during World War II*

And, my summers at my European relatives' farm in Michigan, during my childhood years...

Author's great-grandmother, in background; mother, right, and myself, left at the age of about seven

*Author's mother at home in village of
two thousand in Minnesota when he
was fourteen*

To Contact the Author...

The author welcomes any and all comments and suggestions, and would very much enjoy chatting with you....

message@goldpogo.com

Author

Mt Mitchell North Carolina

Author a couple of years' back...

REFUND POLICY

REFUND INFORMATION

Desire a refund? No problem: 100% refund, for any reason at all, and absolutely no questions asked, period. And no time limit on this offer. I recognize that sometimes, purchased items are discovered to simply not be a "good fit", or for any number of other reasons,...

Loran Joly

If for any reason you desire a refund or desire to leave a comment,

please contact me at:

message@goldpogo.com

or

ReEnvision Press
Box #1036
1303 US 127 South
Suite 104
Frankfort, KY 40601